KEEPING ON TRACK

—— WITH MY ——

FITNESS GOALS

Fitness Journal

ACTIVINOTES

Activinotes

DAILY JOURNALS, PLANNERS, NOTEBOOKS AND OTHER BLANK BOOKS

DATE: ___/___/_____

STRENGTH TRAINING

EXERCISE	SET 1	SET 2	SET 3	SET 4	SET5

Time Start: Time Stop:

CARDIO

EXERCISE	TIME	INTENSITY	DISTANCE	RATE	CALORIES

Time Start: Time Stop:

CLASS	TIME		FLEXIBILITY	TIME

NOTES

FOOD LOG

BREAKFAST	NOTES

SNACK	NOTES

LUNCH	NOTES

SNACK	NOTES

DINNER	NOTES

NUTRIENT TRACKER

	# OF SERVINGS						
GRAIN							
VEGGIES							
FRUITS							
DAIRY							
PROTEIN							
FATS							
VITAMINS							
SUGAR							

NOTES

HOURS OF SLEEP: _____

GLASSES OF WATER FOR TODAY : _____

DATE: ___/___/_____

STRENGTH TRAINING		Time Start:		Time Stop:		
EXERCISE	SET 1	SET 2	SET 3	SET 4	SET5

CARDIO		Time Start:		Time Stop:		
EXERCISE	TIME	INTENSITY	DISTANCE	RATE	CALORIES

CLASS	TIME	FLEXIBILITY	TIME

NOTES

FOOD LOG

BREAKFAST	NOTES

SNACK	NOTES

LUNCH	NOTES

SNACK	NOTES

DINNER	NOTES

NUTRIENT TRACKER

	# OF SERVINGS						
GRAIN							
VEGGIES							
FRUITS							
DAIRY							
PROTEIN							
FATS							
VITAMINS							
SUGAR							

NOTES

HOURS OF SLEEP: _____

GLASSES OF WATER FOR TODAY : _____

DATE: ___/___/_____

STRENGTH TRAINING   Time Start: Time Stop:

EXERCISE	SET 1	SET 2	SET 3	SET 4	SET5

CARDIO   Time Start: Time Stop:

EXERCISE	TIME	INTENSITY	DISTANCE	RATE	CALORIES

CLASS	TIME

FLEXIBILITY	TIME

NOTES

FOOD LOG

BREAKFAST	NOTES

SNACK	NOTES

LUNCH	NOTES

SNACK	NOTES

DINNER	NOTES

NUTRIENT TRACKER

	# OF SERVINGS						
GRAIN							
VEGGIES							
FRUITS							
DAIRY							
PROTEIN							
FATS							
VITAMINS							
SUGAR							

NOTES

HOURS OF SLEEP: _____

GLASSES OF WATER FOR TODAY : _____

DATE: ___/___/____

STRENGTH TRAINING

EXERCISE	Time Start:			Time Stop:	
	SET 1	SET 2	SET 3	SET 4	SET5

CARDIO

EXERCISE	Time Start:		Time Stop:		
	TIME	INTENSITY	DISTANCE	RATE	CALORIES

CLASS	TIME

FLEXIBILITY	TIME

NOTES

FOOD LOG

BREAKFAST	NOTES

SNACK	NOTES

LUNCH	NOTES

SNACK	NOTES

DINNER	NOTES

NUTRIENT TRACKER

	# OF SERVINGS						
GRAIN							
VEGGIES							
FRUITS							
DAIRY							
PROTEIN							
FATS							
VITAMINS							
SUGAR							

NOTES

HOURS OF SLEEP: _____

GLASSES OF WATER FOR TODAY : _____

DATE: ___/___/_____

STRENGTH TRAINING

EXERCISE	SET 1	SET 2	SET 3	SET 4	SET5
Time Start:				Time Stop:	

CARDIO

EXERCISE	TIME	INTENSITY	DISTANCE	RATE	CALORIES
Time Start:			Time Stop:		

CLASS	TIME		FLEXIBILITY	TIME

NOTES

FOOD LOG

BREAKFAST	NOTES

SNACK	NOTES

LUNCH	NOTES

SNACK	NOTES

DINNER	NOTES

NUTRIENT TRACKER

	# OF SERVINGS						
GRAIN							
VEGGIES							
FRUITS							
DAIRY							
PROTEIN							
FATS							
VITAMINS							
SUGAR							

HOURS OF SLEEP: _____

GLASSES OF WATER FOR TODAY : _____

NOTES

DATE: ___/___/____

STRENGTH TRAINING		Time Start:		Time Stop:	
EXERCISE	**SET 1**	**SET 2**	**SET 3**	**SET 4**	**SET5**

CARDIO		Time Start:		Time Stop:	
EXERCISE	**TIME**	**INTENSITY**	**DISTANCE**	**RATE**	**CALORIES**

CLASS	TIME

FLEXIBILITY	TIME

NOTES

FOOD LOG

BREAKFAST	NOTES

SNACK	NOTES

LUNCH	NOTES

SNACK	NOTES

DINNER	NOTES

NUTRIENT TRACKER

	# OF SERVINGS						
GRAIN							
VEGGIES							
FRUITS							
DAIRY							
PROTEIN							
FATS							
VITAMINS							
SUGAR							

NOTES

HOURS OF SLEEP: _____

GLASSES OF WATER FOR TODAY : _____

DATE: ___/___/_____

STRENGTH TRAINING   Time Start: Time Stop:

EXERCISE	SET 1	SET 2	SET 3	SET 4	SET5

CARDIO   Time Start: Time Stop:

EXERCISE	TIME	INTENSITY	DISTANCE	RATE	CALORIES

CLASS	TIME

FLEXIBILITY	TIME

NOTES

FOOD LOG

BREAKFAST	NOTES

SNACK	NOTES

LUNCH	NOTES

SNACK	NOTES

DINNER	NOTES

NUTRIENT TRACKER

	# OF SERVINGS						
GRAIN							
VEGGIES							
FRUITS							
DAIRY							
PROTEIN							
FATS							
VITAMINS							
SUGAR							

NOTES

HOURS OF SLEEP: _____
GLASSES OF WATER FOR TODAY : _____

DATE: ___/___/____

STRENGTH TRAINING   Time Start: Time Stop:

EXERCISE	SET 1	SET 2	SET 3	SET 4	SET5

CARDIO   Time Start: Time Stop:

EXERCISE	TIME	INTENSITY	DISTANCE	RATE	CALORIES

CLASS	TIME

FLEXIBILITY	TIME

NOTES

FOOD LOG

BREAKFAST	NOTES

SNACK	NOTES

LUNCH	NOTES

SNACK	NOTES

DINNER	NOTES

NUTRIENT TRACKER

	# OF SERVINGS						
GRAIN							
VEGGIES							
FRUITS							
DAIRY							
PROTEIN							
FATS							
VITAMINS							
SUGAR							

HOURS OF SLEEP: _____

GLASSES OF WATER FOR TODAY : _____

NOTES

DATE: ___/___/_____

STRENGTH TRAINING

Time Start: Time Stop:

EXERCISE	SET 1	SET 2	SET 3	SET 4	SET5

CARDIO

Time Start: Time Stop:

EXERCISE	TIME	INTENSITY	DISTANCE	RATE	CALORIES

CLASS	TIME

FLEXIBILITY	TIME

NOTES

FOOD LOG

BREAKFAST	NOTES

SNACK	NOTES

LUNCH	NOTES

SNACK	NOTES

DINNER	NOTES

NUTRIENT TRACKER

	# OF SERVINGS						
GRAIN							
VEGGIES							
FRUITS							
DAIRY							
PROTEIN							
FATS							
VITAMINS							
SUGAR							

NOTES

HOURS OF SLEEP: _____

GLASSES OF WATER FOR TODAY : _____

DATE: ___/___/_____

STRENGTH TRAINING	Time Start:		Time Stop:		
EXERCISE	SET 1	SET 2	SET 3	SET 4	SET5

CARDIO	Time Start:		Time Stop:		
EXERCISE	TIME	INTENSITY	DISTANCE	RATE	CALORIES

CLASS	TIME

FLEXIBILITY	TIME

NOTES

FOOD LOG

BREAKFAST	NOTES

SNACK	NOTES

LUNCH	NOTES

SNACK	NOTES

DINNER	NOTES

NUTRIENT TRACKER

	# OF SERVINGS						
GRAIN							
VEGGIES							
FRUITS							
DAIRY							
PROTEIN							
FATS							
VITAMINS							
SUGAR							

NOTES

HOURS OF SLEEP: _____

GLASSES OF WATER FOR TODAY : _____

DATE: ___/___/____

STRENGTH TRAINING   Time Start: Time Stop:

EXERCISE	SET 1	SET 2	SET 3	SET 4	SET5

CARDIO   Time Start: Time Stop:

EXERCISE	TIME	INTENSITY	DISTANCE	RATE	CALORIES

CLASS	TIME

FLEXIBILITY	TIME

NOTES

FOOD LOG

BREAKFAST	NOTES

SNACK	NOTES

LUNCH	NOTES

SNACK	NOTES

DINNER	NOTES

NUTRIENT TRACKER

	# OF SERVINGS						
GRAIN							
VEGGIES							
FRUITS							
DAIRY							
PROTEIN							
FATS							
VITAMINS							
SUGAR							

NOTES

HOURS OF SLEEP: _____

GLASSES OF WATER FOR TODAY : _____

DATE: ___/___/_____

STRENGTH TRAINING		Time Start:		Time Stop:	
EXERCISE	SET 1	SET 2	SET 3	SET 4	SET5

CARDIO		Time Start:		Time Stop:	
EXERCISE	TIME	INTENSITY	DISTANCE	RATE	CALORIES

CLASS	TIME

FLEXIBILITY	TIME

NOTES

FOOD LOG

BREAKFAST	NOTES

SNACK	NOTES

LUNCH	NOTES

SNACK	NOTES

DINNER	NOTES

NUTRIENT TRACKER

	# OF SERVINGS						
GRAIN							
VEGGIES							
FRUITS							
DAIRY							
PROTEIN							
FATS							
VITAMINS							
SUGAR							

HOURS OF SLEEP: _____
GLASSES OF WATER FOR TODAY : _____

NOTES

DATE: ___/___/_____

STRENGTH TRAINING   Time Start: Time Stop:

EXERCISE	SET 1	SET 2	SET 3	SET 4	SET5

CARDIO   Time Start: Time Stop:

EXERCISE	TIME	INTENSITY	DISTANCE	RATE	CALORIES

CLASS TIME	FLEXIBILITY TIME

NOTES

FOOD LOG

BREAKFAST	NOTES

SNACK	NOTES

LUNCH	NOTES

SNACK	NOTES

DINNER	NOTES

NUTRIENT TRACKER

	# OF SERVINGS						
GRAIN							
VEGGIES							
FRUITS							
DAIRY							
PROTEIN							
FATS							
VITAMINS							
SUGAR							

NOTES

HOURS OF SLEEP: _____

GLASSES OF WATER FOR TODAY : _____

DATE: ___/___/_____

STRENGTH TRAINING		Time Start:		Time Stop:	
EXERCISE	**SET 1**	**SET 2**	**SET 3**	**SET 4**	**SET5**

CARDIO		Time Start:		Time Stop:	
EXERCISE	**TIME**	**INTENSITY**	**DISTANCE**	**RATE**	**CALORIES**

CLASS	TIME

FLEXIBILITY	TIME

NOTES

FOOD LOG

BREAKFAST	NOTES

SNACK	NOTES

LUNCH	NOTES

SNACK	NOTES

DINNER	NOTES

NUTRIENT TRACKER

	# OF SERVINGS						
GRAIN							
VEGGIES							
FRUITS							
DAIRY							
PROTEIN							
FATS							
VITAMINS							
SUGAR							

NOTES

HOURS OF SLEEP: _____

GLASSES OF WATER FOR TODAY : _____

DATE: ___/___/_____

STRENGTH TRAINING

Time Start: Time Stop:

EXERCISE	SET 1	SET 2	SET 3	SET 4	SET5

CARDIO

Time Start: Time Stop:

EXERCISE	TIME	INTENSITY	DISTANCE	RATE	CALORIES

CLASS	TIME		FLEXIBILITY	TIME

NOTES

FOOD LOG

BREAKFAST	NOTES

SNACK	NOTES

LUNCH	NOTES

SNACK	NOTES

DINNER	NOTES

NUTRIENT TRACKER

	# OF SERVINGS						
GRAIN							
VEGGIES							
FRUITS							
DAIRY							
PROTEIN							
FATS							
VITAMINS							
SUGAR							

NOTES

HOURS OF SLEEP: _____

GLASSES OF WATER FOR TODAY : _____

DATE: ___/___/____

STRENGTH TRAINING

EXERCISE	SET 1	SET 2	SET 3	SET 4	SET5

Time Start: Time Stop:

CARDIO

EXERCISE	TIME	INTENSITY	DISTANCE	RATE	CALORIES

Time Start: Time Stop:

CLASS	TIME

FLEXIBILITY	TIME

NOTES

FOOD LOG

BREAKFAST	NOTES

SNACK	NOTES

LUNCH	NOTES

SNACK	NOTES

DINNER	NOTES

NUTRIENT TRACKER

	# OF SERVINGS						
GRAIN							
VEGGIES							
FRUITS							
DAIRY							
PROTEIN							
FATS							
VITAMINS							
SUGAR							

HOURS OF SLEEP: _____

GLASSES OF WATER FOR TODAY : _____

NOTES

DATE: ___/___/_____

STRENGTH TRAINING		Time Start:		Time Stop:		
EXERCISE	SET 1	SET 2	SET 3	SET 4	SET5

CARDIO		Time Start:		Time Stop:		
EXERCISE	TIME	INTENSITY	DISTANCE	RATE	CALORIES

CLASS	TIME		FLEXIBILITY	TIME

NOTES

FOOD LOG

BREAKFAST	NOTES

SNACK	NOTES

LUNCH	NOTES

SNACK	NOTES

DINNER	NOTES

NUTRIENT TRACKER

	# OF SERVINGS						
GRAIN							
VEGGIES							
FRUITS							
DAIRY							
PROTEIN							
FATS							
VITAMINS							
SUGAR							

NOTES

HOURS OF SLEEP: _____

GLASSES OF WATER FOR TODAY : _____

DATE: ___/___/_____

STRENGTH TRAINING

	Time Start:			Time Stop:	
EXERCISE	SET 1	SET 2	SET 3	SET 4	SET5

CARDIO

	Time Start:			Time Stop:	
EXERCISE	TIME	INTENSITY	DISTANCE	RATE	CALORIES

CLASS	TIME

FLEXIBILITY	TIME

NOTES

FOOD LOG

BREAKFAST	NOTES

SNACK	NOTES

LUNCH	NOTES

SNACK	NOTES

DINNER	NOTES

NUTRIENT TRACKER

	# OF SERVINGS						
GRAIN							
VEGGIES							
FRUITS							
DAIRY							
PROTEIN							
FATS							
VITAMINS							
SUGAR							

HOURS OF SLEEP: _____

GLASSES OF WATER FOR TODAY : _____

NOTES

DATE: ___/___/_____

STRENGTH TRAINING

EXERCISE	SET 1	SET 2	SET 3	SET 4	SET5

Time Start: Time Stop:

CARDIO

Time Start: Time Stop:

EXERCISE	TIME	INTENSITY	DISTANCE	RATE	CALORIES

CLASS	TIME

FLEXIBILITY	TIME

NOTES

FOOD LOG

BREAKFAST	NOTES

SNACK	NOTES

LUNCH	NOTES

SNACK	NOTES

DINNER	NOTES

NUTRIENT TRACKER

	# OF SERVINGS						
GRAIN							
VEGGIES							
FRUITS							
DAIRY							
PROTEIN							
FATS							
VITAMINS							
SUGAR							

NOTES

HOURS OF SLEEP: _____

GLASSES OF WATER FOR TODAY : _____

DATE: ___/___/_____

STRENGTH TRAINING — Time Start: — Time Stop:

EXERCISE	SET 1	SET 2	SET 3	SET 4	SET5

CARDIO — Time Start: — Time Stop:

EXERCISE	TIME	INTENSITY	DISTANCE	RATE	CALORIES

CLASS	TIME

FLEXIBILITY	TIME

NOTES

FOOD LOG	
BREAKFAST	**NOTES**
SNACK	**NOTES**
LUNCH	**NOTES**
SNACK	**NOTES**
DINNER	**NOTES**

NUTRIENT TRACKER

	# OF SERVINGS						
GRAIN							
VEGGIES							
FRUITS							
DAIRY							
PROTEIN							
FATS							
VITAMINS							
SUGAR							

NOTES

HOURS OF SLEEP: _____

GLASSES OF WATER FOR TODAY : _____

DATE: ___/___/_____

STRENGTH TRAINING

EXERCISE	Time Start:		Time Stop:		
	SET 1	SET 2	SET 3	SET 4	SET5

CARDIO

EXERCISE	Time Start:		Time Stop:		
	TIME	INTENSITY	DISTANCE	RATE	CALORIES

CLASS	TIME	FLEXIBILITY	TIME

NOTES

FOOD LOG

BREAKFAST
NOTES

SNACK
NOTES

LUNCH
NOTES

SNACK
NOTES

DINNER
NOTES

NUTRIENT TRACKER

	# OF SERVINGS							
GRAIN								
VEGGIES								
FRUITS								
DAIRY								
PROTEIN								
FATS								
VITAMINS								
SUGAR								

NOTES

HOURS OF SLEEP: _____

GLASSES OF WATER FOR TODAY : _____

DATE: ___/___/_____

STRENGTH TRAINING		Time Start:			Time Stop:	
EXERCISE	SET 1	SET 2	SET 3	SET 4	SET5

CARDIO		Time Start:		Time Stop:		
EXERCISE	TIME	INTENSITY	DISTANCE	RATE	CALORIES

CLASS	TIME

FLEXIBILITY	TIME

NOTES

FOOD LOG

BREAKFAST	NOTES

SNACK	NOTES

LUNCH	NOTES

SNACK	NOTES

DINNER	NOTES

NUTRIENT TRACKER

	# OF SERVINGS						
GRAIN							
VEGGIES							
FRUITS							
DAIRY							
PROTEIN							
FATS							
VITAMINS							
SUGAR							

HOURS OF SLEEP: _____

GLASSES OF WATER FOR TODAY : _____

NOTES

DATE: ___/___/_____

STRENGTH TRAINING						
EXERCISE		SET 1	SET 2	SET 3	SET 4	SET5

Time Start: Time Stop:

CARDIO						
EXERCISE		TIME	INTENSITY	DISTANCE	RATE	CALORIES

Time Start: Time Stop:

CLASS	TIME

FLEXIBILITY	TIME

NOTES

FOOD LOG	
BREAKFAST	**NOTES**
SNACK	**NOTES**
LUNCH	**NOTES**
SNACK	**NOTES**
DINNER	**NOTES**

NUTRIENT TRACKER

	# OF SERVINGS							
GRAIN								
VEGGIES								
FRUITS								
DAIRY								
PROTEIN								
FATS								
VITAMINS								
SUGAR								

NOTES

HOURS OF SLEEP: _____
GLASSES OF WATER FOR TODAY : _____

DATE: ___/___/_____

STRENGTH TRAINING	Time Start:		Time Stop:		
EXERCISE	SET 1	SET 2	SET 3	SET 4	SET5

CARDIO	Time Start:		Time Stop:		
EXERCISE	TIME	INTENSITY	DISTANCE	RATE	CALORIES

CLASS	TIME

FLEXIBILITY	TIME

NOTES

FOOD LOG

BREAKFAST	NOTES

SNACK	NOTES

LUNCH	NOTES

SNACK	NOTES

DINNER	NOTES

NUTRIENT TRACKER

	# OF SERVINGS						
GRAIN							
VEGGIES							
FRUITS							
DAIRY							
PROTEIN							
FATS							
VITAMINS							
SUGAR							

NOTES

HOURS OF SLEEP: _____

GLASSES OF WATER FOR TODAY : _____

DATE: ___/___/_____

STRENGTH TRAINING	Time Start:		Time Stop:		
EXERCISE	SET 1	SET 2	SET 3	SET 4	SET5

CARDIO	Time Start:		Time Stop:		
EXERCISE	TIME	INTENSITY	DISTANCE	RATE	CALORIES

CLASS	TIME	FLEXIBILITY	TIME

NOTES

FOOD LOG

BREAKFAST	NOTES

SNACK	NOTES

LUNCH	NOTES

SNACK	NOTES

DINNER	NOTES

NUTRIENT TRACKER

	# OF SERVINGS						
GRAIN							
VEGGIES							
FRUITS							
DAIRY							
PROTEIN							
FATS							
VITAMINS							
SUGAR							

HOURS OF SLEEP: _____
GLASSES OF WATER FOR TODAY : _____

NOTES

DATE: ___/___/_____

STRENGTH TRAINING		Time Start:		Time Stop:	
EXERCISE	SET 1	SET 2	SET 3	SET 4	SET5

CARDIO		Time Start:		Time Stop:	
EXERCISE	TIME	INTENSITY	DISTANCE	RATE	CALORIES

CLASS	TIME		FLEXIBILITY	TIME

NOTES

FOOD LOG

BREAKFAST	NOTES

SNACK	NOTES

LUNCH	NOTES

SNACK	NOTES

DINNER	NOTES

NUTRIENT TRACKER

	# OF SERVINGS							
GRAIN								
VEGGIES								
FRUITS								
DAIRY								
PROTEIN								
FATS								
VITAMINS								
SUGAR								

HOURS OF SLEEP: _____

GLASSES OF WATER FOR TODAY : _____

NOTES

DATE: ___/___/_____

STRENGTH TRAINING					
EXERCISE	SET 1	SET 2	SET 3	SET 4	SET5

Time Start: Time Stop:

CARDIO					
EXERCISE	TIME	INTENSITY	DISTANCE	RATE	CALORIES

Time Start: Time Stop:

CLASS	TIME

FLEXIBILITY	TIME

NOTES

FOOD LOG

BREAKFAST	NOTES

SNACK	NOTES

LUNCH	NOTES

SNACK	NOTES

DINNER	NOTES

NUTRIENT TRACKER

	# OF SERVINGS						
GRAIN							
VEGGIES							
FRUITS							
DAIRY							
PROTEIN							
FATS							
VITAMINS							
SUGAR							

NOTES

HOURS OF SLEEP: _____

GLASSES OF WATER FOR TODAY : _____

DATE: ___/___/____

STRENGTH TRAINING		Time Start:		Time Stop:	
EXERCISE	SET 1	SET 2	SET 3	SET 4	SET5

CARDIO		Time Start:		Time Stop:	
EXERCISE	TIME	INTENSITY	DISTANCE	RATE	CALORIES

CLASS	TIME	FLEXIBILITY	TIME

NOTES

FOOD LOG

BREAKFAST	NOTES

SNACK	NOTES

LUNCH	NOTES

SNACK	NOTES

DINNER	NOTES

NUTRIENT TRACKER

	# OF SERVINGS							
GRAIN								
VEGGIES								
FRUITS								
DAIRY								
PROTEIN								
FATS								
VITAMINS								
SUGAR								

NOTES

HOURS OF SLEEP: _____

GLASSES OF WATER FOR TODAY : _____

DATE: ___/___/_____

STRENGTH TRAINING

EXERCISE	SET 1	SET 2	SET 3	SET 4	SET5

Time Start: Time Stop:

CARDIO

EXERCISE	TIME	INTENSITY	DISTANCE	RATE	CALORIES

Time Start: Time Stop:

CLASS	TIME

FLEXIBILITY	TIME

NOTES

FOOD LOG

BREAKFAST	NOTES

SNACK	NOTES

LUNCH	NOTES

SNACK	NOTES

DINNER	NOTES

NUTRIENT TRACKER

	# OF SERVINGS						
GRAIN							
VEGGIES							
FRUITS							
DAIRY							
PROTEIN							
FATS							
VITAMINS							
SUGAR							

NOTES

HOURS OF SLEEP: _____

GLASSES OF WATER FOR TODAY : _____

DATE: ___/___/_____

STRENGTH TRAINING		Time Start:		Time Stop:	
EXERCISE	**SET 1**	**SET 2**	**SET 3**	**SET 4**	**SET5**

CARDIO		Time Start:		Time Stop:	
EXERCISE	**TIME**	**INTENSITY**	**DISTANCE**	**RATE**	**CALORIES**

CLASS	TIME		FLEXIBILITY	TIME

NOTES

FOOD LOG

BREAKFAST	NOTES

SNACK	NOTES

LUNCH	NOTES

SNACK	NOTES

DINNER	NOTES

NUTRIENT TRACKER

	# OF SERVINGS						
GRAIN							
VEGGIES							
FRUITS							
DAIRY							
PROTEIN							
FATS							
VITAMINS							
SUGAR							

NOTES

HOURS OF SLEEP: _____

GLASSES OF WATER FOR TODAY : _____

DATE: ___/___/_____

STRENGTH TRAINING		Time Start:			Time Stop:	
EXERCISE	SET 1	SET 2	SET 3	SET 4	SET5

CARDIO		Time Start:		Time Stop:		
EXERCISE	TIME	INTENSITY	DISTANCE	RATE	CALORIES

CLASS	TIME

FLEXIBILITY	TIME

NOTES

FOOD LOG

BREAKFAST	NOTES
SNACK	NOTES
LUNCH	NOTES
SNACK	NOTES
DINNER	NOTES

NUTRIENT TRACKER

	# OF SERVINGS						
GRAIN							
VEGGIES							
FRUITS							
DAIRY							
PROTEIN							
FATS							
VITAMINS							
SUGAR							

NOTES

HOURS OF SLEEP: _____

GLASSES OF WATER FOR TODAY : _____

DATE: ___/___/_____

STRENGTH TRAINING		Time Start:		Time Stop:	
EXERCISE	SET 1	SET 2	SET 3	SET 4	SET5

CARDIO		Time Start:		Time Stop:	
EXERCISE	TIME	INTENSITY	DISTANCE	RATE	CALORIES

CLASS	TIME	FLEXIBILITY	TIME

NOTES

FOOD LOG

BREAKFAST	NOTES

SNACK	NOTES

LUNCH	NOTES

SNACK	NOTES

DINNER	NOTES

NUTRIENT TRACKER

	# OF SERVINGS						
GRAIN							
VEGGIES							
FRUITS							
DAIRY							
PROTEIN							
FATS							
VITAMINS							
SUGAR							

HOURS OF SLEEP: _____

GLASSES OF WATER FOR TODAY : _____

NOTES

DATE: ___/___/_____

STRENGTH TRAINING   Time Start: Time Stop:

EXERCISE	SET 1	SET 2	SET 3	SET 4	SET5

CARDIO   Time Start: Time Stop:

EXERCISE	TIME	INTENSITY	DISTANCE	RATE	CALORIES

CLASS	TIME

FLEXIBILITY	TIME

NOTES

FOOD LOG

BREAKFAST	NOTES

SNACK	NOTES

LUNCH	NOTES

SNACK	NOTES

DINNER	NOTES

NUTRIENT TRACKER

NOTES

	# OF SERVINGS						
GRAIN							
VEGGIES							
FRUITS							
DAIRY							
PROTEIN							
FATS							
VITAMINS							
SUGAR							

HOURS OF SLEEP: _____

GLASSES OF WATER FOR TODAY : _____

DATE: ___/___/_____

STRENGTH TRAINING		Time Start:		Time Stop:	
EXERCISE	**SET 1**	**SET 2**	**SET 3**	**SET 4**	**SET5**

CARDIO		Time Start:		Time Stop:	
EXERCISE	**TIME**	**INTENSITY**	**DISTANCE**	**RATE**	**CALORIES**

CLASS	TIME		FLEXIBILITY		TIME

NOTES

FOOD LOG

BREAKFAST	NOTES

SNACK	NOTES

LUNCH	NOTES

SNACK	NOTES

DINNER	NOTES

NUTRIENT TRACKER

	# OF SERVINGS						
GRAIN							
VEGGIES							
FRUITS							
DAIRY							
PROTEIN							
FATS							
VITAMINS							
SUGAR							

NOTES

HOURS OF SLEEP: _____

GLASSES OF WATER FOR TODAY : _____

DATE: ___/___/_____

STRENGTH TRAINING

Time Start: Time Stop:

EXERCISE	SET 1	SET 2	SET 3	SET 4	SET5

CARDIO

Time Start: Time Stop:

EXERCISE	TIME	INTENSITY	DISTANCE	RATE	CALORIES

CLASS	TIME		FLEXIBILITY	TIME

NOTES

FOOD LOG

BREAKFAST	NOTES

SNACK	NOTES

LUNCH	NOTES

SNACK	NOTES

DINNER	NOTES

NUTRIENT TRACKER

	# OF SERVINGS						
GRAIN							
VEGGIES							
FRUITS							
DAIRY							
PROTEIN							
FATS							
VITAMINS							
SUGAR							

NOTES

HOURS OF SLEEP: _____
GLASSES OF WATER FOR TODAY : _____

DATE: ___/___/_____

STRENGTH TRAINING

Time Start: Time Stop:

EXERCISE	SET 1	SET 2	SET 3	SET 4	SET5

CARDIO

Time Start: Time Stop:

EXERCISE	TIME	INTENSITY	DISTANCE	RATE	CALORIES

CLASS	TIME

FLEXIBILITY	TIME

NOTES

FOOD LOG

BREAKFAST	NOTES

SNACK	NOTES

LUNCH	NOTES

SNACK	NOTES

DINNER	NOTES

NUTRIENT TRACKER

	# OF SERVINGS						
GRAIN							
VEGGIES							
FRUITS							
DAIRY							
PROTEIN							
FATS							
VITAMINS							
SUGAR							

NOTES

HOURS OF SLEEP: _____

GLASSES OF WATER FOR TODAY : _____

DATE: ___/___/_____

STRENGTH TRAINING

Time Start: **Time Stop:**

EXERCISE	SET 1	SET 2	SET 3	SET 4	SET5

CARDIO

Time Start: **Time Stop:**

EXERCISE	TIME	INTENSITY	DISTANCE	RATE	CALORIES

CLASS	TIME

FLEXIBILITY	TIME

NOTES

FOOD LOG

BREAKFAST	NOTES

SNACK	NOTES

LUNCH	NOTES

SNACK	NOTES

DINNER	NOTES

NUTRIENT TRACKER

	# OF SERVINGS							
GRAIN								
VEGGIES								
FRUITS								
DAIRY								
PROTEIN								
FATS								
VITAMINS								
SUGAR								

NOTES

HOURS OF SLEEP: _____

GLASSES OF WATER FOR TODAY : _____

DATE: ___ / ___ / _____

STRENGTH TRAINING		Time Start:		Time Stop:	
EXERCISE	**SET 1**	**SET 2**	**SET 3**	**SET 4**	**SET5**

CARDIO		Time Start:		Time Stop:	
EXERCISE	**TIME**	**INTENSITY**	**DISTANCE**	**RATE**	**CALORIES**

CLASS	TIME

FLEXIBILITY	TIME

NOTES

FOOD LOG

BREAKFAST	NOTES

SNACK	NOTES

LUNCH	NOTES

SNACK	NOTES

DINNER	NOTES

NUTRIENT TRACKER

	# OF SERVINGS						
GRAIN							
VEGGIES							
FRUITS							
DAIRY							
PROTEIN							
FATS							
VITAMINS							
SUGAR							

NOTES

HOURS OF SLEEP: _____

GLASSES OF WATER FOR TODAY : _____

DATE: ___/___/_____

STRENGTH TRAINING — Time Start: ___ Time Stop: ___

EXERCISE	SET 1	SET 2	SET 3	SET 4	SET5

CARDIO — Time Start: ___ Time Stop: ___

EXERCISE	TIME	INTENSITY	DISTANCE	RATE	CALORIES

CLASS	TIME

FLEXIBILITY	TIME

NOTES

FOOD LOG

BREAKFAST	NOTES

SNACK	NOTES

LUNCH	NOTES

SNACK	NOTES

DINNER	NOTES

NUTRIENT TRACKER

	# OF SERVINGS						
GRAIN							
VEGGIES							
FRUITS							
DAIRY							
PROTEIN							
FATS							
VITAMINS							
SUGAR							

HOURS OF SLEEP: _____

GLASSES OF WATER FOR TODAY : _____

NOTES

DATE: ___/___/_____

STRENGTH TRAINING			Time Start:		Time Stop:	
EXERCISE	**SET 1**	**SET 2**	**SET 3**	**SET 4**	**SET5**

CARDIO			Time Start:		Time Stop:	
EXERCISE	**TIME**	**INTENSITY**	**DISTANCE**	**RATE**	**CALORIES**

CLASS	TIME

FLEXIBILITY	TIME

NOTES

FOOD LOG

BREAKFAST	NOTES

SNACK	NOTES

LUNCH	NOTES

SNACK	NOTES

DINNER	NOTES

NUTRIENT TRACKER

	# OF SERVINGS						
GRAIN							
VEGGIES							
FRUITS							
DAIRY							
PROTEIN							
FATS							
VITAMINS							
SUGAR							

NOTES

HOURS OF SLEEP: _____

GLASSES OF WATER FOR TODAY : _____

DATE: ___/___/_____

STRENGTH TRAINING

EXERCISE	SET 1	SET 2	SET 3	SET 4	SET5

Time Start: Time Stop:

CARDIO

EXERCISE	TIME	INTENSITY	DISTANCE	RATE	CALORIES

Time Start: Time Stop:

CLASS	TIME

FLEXIBILITY	TIME

NOTES

FOOD LOG	
BREAKFAST	**NOTES**
SNACK	**NOTES**
LUNCH	**NOTES**
SNACK	**NOTES**
DINNER	**NOTES**

NUTRIENT TRACKER

	# OF SERVINGS						
GRAIN							
VEGGIES							
FRUITS							
DAIRY							
PROTEIN							
FATS							
VITAMINS							
SUGAR							

NOTES

HOURS OF SLEEP: _____

GLASSES OF WATER FOR TODAY : _____

DATE: ___/___/_____

STRENGTH TRAINING		Time Start:		Time Stop:	
EXERCISE	SET 1	SET 2	SET 3	SET 4	SET5

CARDIO		Time Start:		Time Stop:	
EXERCISE	TIME	INTENSITY	DISTANCE	RATE	CALORIES

CLASS	TIME		FLEXIBILITY	TIME

NOTES

FOOD LOG

BREAKFAST	NOTES

SNACK	NOTES

LUNCH	NOTES

SNACK	NOTES

DINNER	NOTES

NUTRIENT TRACKER

	# OF SERVINGS						
GRAIN							
VEGGIES							
FRUITS							
DAIRY							
PROTEIN							
FATS							
VITAMINS							
SUGAR							

NOTES

HOURS OF SLEEP: _____

GLASSES OF WATER FOR TODAY : _____

DATE: ___/___/_____

STRENGTH TRAINING

EXERCISE	Time Start:	Time Stop:			
	SET 1	SET 2	SET 3	SET 4	SET5

CARDIO

EXERCISE	Time Start:	Time Stop:			
	TIME	INTENSITY	DISTANCE	RATE	CALORIES

CLASS	TIME		FLEXIBILITY	TIME

NOTES

FOOD LOG

BREAKFAST	NOTES

SNACK	NOTES

LUNCH	NOTES

SNACK	NOTES

DINNER	NOTES

NUTRIENT TRACKER

	# OF SERVINGS						
GRAIN							
VEGGIES							
FRUITS							
DAIRY							
PROTEIN							
FATS							
VITAMINS							
SUGAR							

NOTES

HOURS OF SLEEP: _____

GLASSES OF WATER FOR TODAY : _____

DATE: ___/___/____

STRENGTH TRAINING   Time Start: Time Stop:

EXERCISE	SET 1	SET 2	SET 3	SET 4	SET5

CARDIO   Time Start: Time Stop:

EXERCISE	TIME	INTENSITY	DISTANCE	RATE	CALORIES

CLASS	TIME

FLEXIBILITY	TIME

NOTES

FOOD LOG

BREAKFAST	NOTES

SNACK	NOTES

LUNCH	NOTES

SNACK	NOTES

DINNER	NOTES

NUTRIENT TRACKER

	# OF SERVINGS						
GRAIN							
VEGGIES							
FRUITS							
DAIRY							
PROTEIN							
FATS							
VITAMINS							
SUGAR							

NOTES

HOURS OF SLEEP: _____

GLASSES OF WATER FOR TODAY : _____

DATE: ___/___/_____

STRENGTH TRAINING

EXERCISE	SET 1	SET 2	SET 3	SET 4	SET5

Time Start: Time Stop:

CARDIO

Time Start: Time Stop:

EXERCISE	TIME	INTENSITY	DISTANCE	RATE	CALORIES

CLASS	TIME

FLEXIBILITY	TIME

NOTES

FOOD LOG	
BREAKFAST	**NOTES**
SNACK	**NOTES**
LUNCH	**NOTES**
SNACK	**NOTES**
DINNER	**NOTES**

NUTRIENT TRACKER

	# OF SERVINGS						
GRAIN							
VEGGIES							
FRUITS							
DAIRY							
PROTEIN							
FATS							
VITAMINS							
SUGAR							

HOURS OF SLEEP: _____

GLASSES OF WATER FOR TODAY : _____

NOTES

DATE: ___/___/_____

STRENGTH TRAINING   Time Start: Time Stop:

EXERCISE	SET 1	SET 2	SET 3	SET 4	SET5

CARDIO   Time Start: Time Stop:

EXERCISE	TIME	INTENSITY	DISTANCE	RATE	CALORIES

CLASS	TIME	FLEXIBILITY	TIME

NOTES

FOOD LOG

BREAKFAST	NOTES

SNACK	NOTES

LUNCH	NOTES

SNACK	NOTES

DINNER	NOTES

NUTRIENT TRACKER

NOTES

	# OF SERVINGS						
GRAIN							
VEGGIES							
FRUITS							
DAIRY							
PROTEIN							
FATS							
VITAMINS							
SUGAR							

HOURS OF SLEEP: _____

GLASSES OF WATER FOR TODAY : _____

DATE: ___/___/_____

STRENGTH TRAINING

Time Start: **Time Stop:**

EXERCISE	SET 1	SET 2	SET 3	SET 4	SET5

CARDIO

Time Start: **Time Stop:**

EXERCISE	TIME	INTENSITY	DISTANCE	RATE	CALORIES

CLASS	TIME

FLEXIBILITY	TIME

NOTES

FOOD LOG

BREAKFAST	NOTES

SNACK	NOTES

LUNCH	NOTES

SNACK	NOTES

DINNER	NOTES

NUTRIENT TRACKER

	# OF SERVINGS						
GRAIN							
VEGGIES							
FRUITS							
DAIRY							
PROTEIN							
FATS							
VITAMINS							
SUGAR							

NOTES

HOURS OF SLEEP: _____

GLASSES OF WATER FOR TODAY : _____

DATE: ___/___/_____

STRENGTH TRAINING	Time Start:		Time Stop:		
EXERCISE	SET 1	SET 2	SET 3	SET 4	SET5

CARDIO	Time Start:		Time Stop:		
EXERCISE	TIME	INTENSITY	DISTANCE	RATE	CALORIES

CLASS	TIME		FLEXIBILITY	TIME

NOTES

FOOD LOG

BREAKFAST	NOTES

SNACK	NOTES

LUNCH	NOTES

SNACK	NOTES

DINNER	NOTES

NUTRIENT TRACKER

	# OF SERVINGS						
GRAIN							
VEGGIES							
FRUITS							
DAIRY							
PROTEIN							
FATS							
VITAMINS							
SUGAR							

NOTES

HOURS OF SLEEP: _____

GLASSES OF WATER FOR TODAY : _____

DATE: ___/___/____

STRENGTH TRAINING		Time Start:		Time Stop:		
EXERCISE	SET 1	SET 2	SET 3	SET 4	SET5

CARDIO		Time Start:		Time Stop:		
EXERCISE	TIME	INTENSITY	DISTANCE	RATE	CALORIES

CLASS	TIME

FLEXIBILITY	TIME

NOTES

FOOD LOG

BREAKFAST	NOTES

SNACK	NOTES

LUNCH	NOTES

SNACK	NOTES

DINNER	NOTES

NUTRIENT TRACKER

	# OF SERVINGS						
GRAIN							
VEGGIES							
FRUITS							
DAIRY							
PROTEIN							
FATS							
VITAMINS							
SUGAR							

NOTES

HOURS OF SLEEP: _____

GLASSES OF WATER FOR TODAY : _____

www.ingramcontent.com/pod-product-compliance
Lightning Source LLC
Chambersburg PA
CBHW080738250626

47170CB00010B/2875